MAKING SENSE
of God's Word

Kenneth Schenck

wesleyan
publishing
house

Indianapolis, Indiana

Copyright © 2009 by Triangle Publishing and Indiana Wesleyan University
Published by Wesleyan Publishing House
Indianapolis, Indiana 46250
Printed in the United States of America
ISBN: 978-0-89827-376-2

Library of Congress Cataloging-in-Publication Data

Schenck, Kenneth, 1966-
  Making sense of God's Word / Kenneth Schenck.
      p. cm.
  Rev. ed. of: Brief guide to biblical interpretation.
  ISBN 978-0-89827-376-2
  1. Bible--Hermeneutics. I. Schenck, Kenneth, 1966- Brief guide to
biblical interpretation. II. Title.
  BS476.S324 2009
  220.601--dc22

                          2008043541

Originally published as *Brief Guide to Biblical Interpretation, Second edition*,
© Triangle Publishing, Marion, Indiana, 2008.

CONTENTS

INTRODUCTION

"God said it; I believe it; that settles it for me!"

The spirit of this affirmation is usually right on target. If something is God's will and adheres to God's position on an issue, the case is closed. The Bible allows for questioning, but if God has spoken about something, his answer must be the final answer.

"I, the LORD, do not change" (Mal. 3:6).

Again, Christians usually quote this verse with a godly fervor. In a culture where change is seen as progress and technology gets better and better, we can find ourselves dismissing the old as irrelevant or ignorant. But Christianity bids us believe that God has known everything from the very beginning. He is not growing up or getting better. God has always been an all-knowing authority. We do not know more now than God did when he inspired the Bible.

While there is something to be said for the confidence expressed by these two statements, they are sometimes quoted to reinforce biblical ignorance and to support positions that are not God's. Christians are sometimes too quick to believe they already know what God has said, but you don't really know what God said, unless you know why he said it. To ignore the reasons behind what God said in the past is to not listen to God at all; it is to force the words of the Bible into someone else's way of thinking.

While God remains the same, humanity does not and has not. The Bible reveals that part of the unchanging nature of God is to communicate and relate to the world in terms it can understand. If we pay attention to the Bible, we will see God meeting different people and groups in different ways over time. The same Bible that allowed divorce in Deuteronomy 24:1–4 prohibits it in Matthew 19:7–9. The same Bible that sanctions stoning a man for violating the Sabbath (Num. 15:32–36) tells a different group not to let anyone judge them because they do not keep it (Col. 2:16–17).

God is an incarnate God (cf. John 1:14), a God who took on flesh to reveal himself to humanity. The story of revelation is the story of God meeting people where they are and using categories they understand—stooping to our weakness. It is why Solomon's temple was structured like the pagan temples typical of his day; God was saying something to the people of Israel in terms they could understand.

The most important step in discerning God's voice is to become a person "after God's own heart," and to get in the center of his will. Surely, though, a deeper understanding of how biblical revelation works is nothing to scorn. Such understanding might very well save us from mistaking our thoughts for God's thoughts!

The purpose of this brief guide is to give you a sense of the main issues involved in that process. It is about *hermeneutics*, the theory of interpretation. Hermeneutics asks how our lives relate to the biblical text. How might we move from the text to our lives or from our lives to the text? This is our topic of conversation in the following pages.

WHERE DOES THE BIBLE FIT?

Many Christians make Bible reading a daily discipline. Perhaps they follow a guide to read through the whole Bible in a year. Others move through it more slowly and methodically. Others meet in Bible study groups and work through various passages together. These are all what we call a "text-to-life" approach to the biblical text. You come to the Bible without a topic in mind and try to listen to whatever the passage you are studying happens to say.

Life often causes us to take another approach to the biblical text. It is one driven by need and circumstance. You are facing a crisis or a decision. You are trying to give comfort to someone in distress. A church is divided over an issue, or science has brought up a subject that the biblical authors never could have imagined. This "life-to-text" approach can be an approach of urgency, of greatest need. One may not have time to pursue a rigorous Bible study method in the throes of a crisis. You need a word from God now!

It is easier to set out a method for the text-to-life approach than it is for a life-to-text emergency. Over the years, evangelical scholars have developed a fairly straightforward method for moving from text to life. Much of this short book moves through the various steps you take to do it. You might call this the inductive Bible study method; it tries to draw meaning *out* of the Bible.

First you observe what the text says. Then you interpret the text and figure out what it meant originally. For Christians who believe the Bible holds authority over them, the task of application or appropriation is the final step in the process. You make the jump from the text to life. Observation and interpretation are very significant skills for any reader of the Bible to have. But knowing how to make the final jump to life is the most crucial skill of all, because it is the one that determines how the Bible will impact your life.

Another important skill is that of integration, knowing how to move from individual biblical texts to a sense of what the Bible as a whole teaches. Sometimes one biblical text seems to point in a different direction from other texts in the Bible. As a result, some forms of inductive Bible study have a step in between the interpretation and appropriation of Scripture in which a person connects the various individual teachings of the Bible's books together before making the jump to today. Certainly the ability to integrate all the Bible's teaching is a crucial skill for the Christian who believes God speaks to us through the biblical text.

What skills are most crucial for the person who brings a question or problem for the Bible to solve, the person who goes from life to text? The skills we have just mentioned are still in play, but the emphasis and method of approach is different. For one, these seekers need to know how to locate the relevant texts. They need to know what passages relate most directly to the situation they need to address. If you are facing a failed marriage and need a word from God, you need to know where in the Bible to find the relevant texts on marriage, divorce, and remarriage.

Secondly, they especially need to know how those individual texts fit with each other; they need the skill of integration. Should they place an emphasis on Old Testament passages or New Testament ones? Should they place an emphasis on the words of Jesus or the words of Paul? Are there principles in Scripture that are broader than the topic of marriage that need to be brought into the discussion?

Finally, they need to know how to appropriate the text, how to jump from the text to their own life. This most crucial step in the process is usually the one most neglected in the typical text-to-life approach. For example, a person might think you can simply apply the words of a passage directly to your life without any other step in the process. But sometimes God emphatically does not want us to do this—like when you are reading the passage in Deuteronomy about stoning a rebellious son (Deut. 21:21).

Whether you're moving from life to text or text to life, the appropriation stage can become very complex. We might look at points of continuity and discontinuity between the world of the Bible and our world (how the two worlds are alike and different) so that we can map a course from one to another. We might look at the trajectory of heaven or the new covenant in Christ—what will God's ideal world look like, in other words—and draw a line to ourselves by this path.

Yet we can study all these things and still come up with different conclusions. Clearly we need the Holy Spirit more than all the methods in the world. We especially sense this need when we are moving from our lives to the text. We want the Holy Spirit to jump out at us from the words.

For the last two millennia, the Holy Spirit *has* been jumping out of the text at Christians. Although Christians disagree on many things, the Holy Spirit has brought God's people to a number of common understandings that often shape how we hear the words of the Bible without us even knowing it much of the time. We should not disdain what God has revealed to Christians throughout the ages from the Bible.

The rest of the book proceeds in four movements. First, we will raise some of the issues that come up in the process of connecting ourselves to the biblical text, what are called hermeneutical issues. Then we'll look at observation and interpretation, two key skills in reading the Bible. Thirdly, we'll address two crucial factors we bring with us from our lives to the text: our experiences and the common sense of Christians throughout the ages. Finally, we'll discuss the meeting of life and text and the tasks of integrating and appropriating the biblical texts.

All these movements are complementary and should form a lifelong circle, a hermeneutical circle. We engage in lifelong observation and interpretation of the Bible and, over our lifetime, build up a more integrated sense of what the Bible teaches. But at the same time, we are also moving to the text with the needs and concerns of our lives, and deepening our understanding of the issues with which the Christians of the ages have already dealt. Ideally, we do all these things in communion with the body of Christ, to "work out [our] salvation with fear and trembling" (Phil. 2:12).

chapter 1

HERMENEUTICS
The Theory Behind Interpretation

CONTEXT IS EVERYTHING

Words are incredibly flexible things—they can mean many different things in many different situations. What makes being fired from a job different from getting fired up or firing a gun or lighting a fire? The context! To know what the word *fire* means, you have to know whether you are talking about your job, enthusiasm, a gun range, or camping.

The words of the Bible are no different in this regard. Why do over twenty thousand different Protestant denominations disagree with each other, yet claim to get their core beliefs from the Bible? It is the incredible flexibility of words. If we are not aware of it, then we are bound to assume that the way we see the words is the only way to see the words.

An important distinction in this regard is the difference between the original meaning of the words of the Bible and any other meanings we might see in the words. The original meaning is the meaning a word had to the original author and audience of the book. What did Paul mean when he said a non-Christian might think that people who spoke in tongues were "out of [their] mind" (1 Cor. 14:23)? The word Paul used may have referred to what people experienced who were involved in the *mystery religions* of his day. This is one example of how the original meaning of the Bible has to do with ancient audiences. We do not come equipped with the necessary background knowledge to understand the words of the Bible as they were originally understood.

The idea of *original meaning* is not without complications. No doubt even the audiences of the biblical texts sometimes misunderstood what the original author was trying to say. Further, some of the words of the Bible were first spoken orally and later written down. The words of Jesus can thus have slightly different meanings depending on context. One meaning would be what he originally meant in whatever specific contexts he first spoke them. The second meaning is the various connotations his words took on in the individual gospel accounts. We should not immediately rule out the possibility that God had meanings in mind for the words of which the original authors were not aware.

Nevertheless, the difference between what the words originally meant and how they might strike us is a valid distinction. For example, Judas was not the hero of the gospels, although someone might choose to read the story this way. A certain tribe in Papua, New Guinea, initially responded more favorably to Judas than to Jesus when they first heard the gospel story. In their culture, Judas fit the profile of the type of person they admired, so their cultural glasses led them to read the story differently than any of the gospel writers intended.

Despite the fact that the biblical texts had an original meaning, the biblical words are susceptible to any number of other interpretations that differ from it. These other meanings vary from interpretations that are quite similar to the original meaning, to others that have almost nothing to do with anything the original audiences would have recognized.

Here is an example. When I read about loving my neighbor, I am probably thinking things that are similar in spirit to the original meaning. Nevertheless, how an ancient audience understood what "loving your neighbor" meant is almost certainly different from what we understand it to mean today — and different from when Jesus or the author of Leviticus spoke of it (Lev. 19:18; Luke 10:27). On the other hand, countless sermons every Sunday morning do things with the Bible that, while they may be true, have nothing to do with anything Moses or Isaiah or Paul would recognize as what they were trying to say. Some of the most relevant sermons deviate the most from the original meaning, for the original meaning was not written to be directly relevant to us, but to the ancient audiences to whom they were first spoken.

These observations lead us to three important aspects of reading the Bible in context.

POINT 1: If we read the Bible for what it originally meant, we can see it was written to someone else.

The literal meaning of Deuteronomy or Romans or 1 Thessalonians requires us to recognize that none of the books of the Bible were strictly written to us. As Christians, we believe these books are for us, but they were not written to us. Deuteronomy says, "Hear, O Israel" (Deut. 6:4). The book of Romans says it was written to individuals in Rome (Rom. 1:7). Paul was specifically addressing the church at Thessalonica when he wrote the letter we call 1 Thessalonians (1 Thess. 1:1). No one alive today is one of those whom Romans and 1 Thessalonians originally addressed. Even modern Israel is not the same Israel found in Deuteronomy 6.

POINT 2: The way the original audiences understood the meaning of these words was a function of the way they used and understood words.

When Jesus said that God sends rain on the just and the unjust in Matthew 5:45, the Galilean peasants understood rain as a very positive thing. Further, they had clear ideas of what it might mean to be just or unjust—definitions that came from their world. When Genesis 1 speaks of waters above the sky (Gen. 1:6–8) and stars put in the sky (Gen. 1:14–15), it pictures a universe in which you go up through a layer of stars before reaching primordial waters above them. When Paul wrote of three heavens (2 Cor. 12:2), he thought of three layers of sky as you go straight up toward

God. These should not pose problems for our faith in the Bible. It simply confirms that God is a God who speaks to us in ways we can understand. He speaks to us today in our categories, not in the categories through which our great grandchildren will view the world.

POINT 3: The way we understand words and the world is not the same as the way they did.

In fact, they even differed from each other in this regard. The preceding examples make this point clear. We might return to the example of rain to make the point again (Matt. 5:45). For many years I did not understand the original meaning of God sending rain just because rain in my internal dictionary is not a good thing. "Rain, rain, go away. Please come back another day." I thought the verse meant that God even allowed bad things to happen to good people.

But attention to the words around Matthew's statement (the literary context) as well as to ancient Galilean culture (the social context) at this point in history (the historical context) shows us that this interpretation differs from the original meaning. Rain was a very good thing to farmers in a land that sometimes went without rain. The verse is about how God gives good things even to bad people. We read the Bible differently from the original meaning in subtle ways all the time.

We should probably not assume that the new meanings we see in the words today cannot be from God or even that they are less from God than the original meanings were. Unless God speaks through the words beyond the original meaning, most of us are in trouble much of the time. Even scholars often disagree on what the original meaning was. Nevertheless, the first step toward a deeper and more mature understanding of the Bible is to recognize the crucial and determinative role that context plays in the meaning we see in it.

Different Kinds of Contexts

If context determines meaning, then we need to get some sense of the different kinds of contexts in which words appear and take on different meanings.

The Literary Context. One of the main contexts to consider when you are reading words is the literary context. The immediate literary context includes the words that come before and after the verse or verses you want to interpret. Matthew 2:15 gives us a great case study in what it means to read words both in context and out of context.

In the literary context of Matthew 2, Jesus' family has gone down to Egypt to escape the persecution of Herod the Great. Then after Herod's death, they return to Israel. Matthew 2:15 says that these events happened so that it might be fulfilled "what the Lord had said through the prophet: 'Out of Egypt I called my son.'" The literary context of Matthew leads us to believe that this event in the life of Jesus was the fulfillment of a prophecy from the Scriptures. This is the meaning of Matthew 2:15 as we read it in its literary context.

17

What is so interesting about Matthew's statement is that he himself was reading the Scriptures we now call the Old Testament out of context. Hosea 11:1, the passage that Matthew quotes says, "When *Israel* was a child, I loved him, and *out of Egypt I called my son*. But the more I called Israel, the further they went away from me. They sacrificed to the Baals" (emphasis mine). When we read Hosea 11:1 in context (paying attention to the words that come before and after), we see that Hosea was talking about the exodus of Israel from Egypt, not Jesus.

Further, the words that follow Hosea 11:1 talk about how Israel disobeyed God by serving other gods—certainly nothing that could apply to Jesus. We will consistently find that the meanings Matthew sees in the Old Testament are not quite the same as the original meanings those words had when they were first written. Scholars debate whether Matthew took the contexts of such passages figuratively or whether he had little interest in their original contexts.

Here we find the question of reading the Bible in context in one of its starkest forms. On the one hand, we value what God might have said through both Hosea and Matthew to their original audiences. After all, was that moment not the first moment of inspiration?

At the same time, Matthew implies that God can also speak through spiritual meanings that the Holy Spirit leads us to see in the words. From Matthew's example, such meanings may or may not have any substantial connection to what those words meant originally. Of course we must be careful about using the Bible in this way. Such meanings will only be as valid as the Holy Spirit in the person who hears them. Christians believe Matthew was inspired. The inspiration of other individuals today is less assured. We will discuss various ways to test the spirits in the pages to come.

Beyond the immediate literary context is the broader literary context of a verse or passage, including the book as a whole. For example, some Christians take 1 Corinthians 14:34–35 to mean that women cannot preach in church: "Women should remain silent in the churches. They are not allowed to speak, but must be in submission, as the Law says. If they want to inquire about something, they should ask their own husbands at home; for it is disgraceful for a woman to speak in the church."

But the broader context of 1 Corinthians makes it clear that whatever these verses might refer to, it cannot be spiritual speech such as preaching. If anything, it must mean normal chatter or disruptive question-raising in the middle of worship. We know this because Paul assumes in 1 Corinthians 11:5, without even arguing, that women do pray and prophesy in church: "Every woman who prays or prophesies with her head uncovered dishonors her head." Since Christian prophecy is something you do in public worship, the broader context of 1 Corinthians 14 suggests that these verses do not refer to spiritual speech but only to disruptive, ordinary speech.

Genre. Another important literary context is the genre of the book we are reading. For example, the book of Revelation is an apocalypse, an ancient genre that is no longer in use. When we compare Revelation to other ancient apocalypses, we realize that it both follows and differs from them in interesting ways.

In other apocalypses, a heavenly figure usually comes down to the person having the vision. The same is true of Revelation: Jesus appears to John. In response to the heavenly figure, the visionary usually falls on his face. Again, this is what happens at the beginning of Revelation. Even knowing this much about the apocalyptic genre raises the question of whether the scene at the beginning of Revelation is meant to be symbolic—a standard feature of the genre—or a blow-by-blow account of John's actual experiences.

What is interesting is that in other apocalypses, the heavenly figure then tells the visionary to get up because only God is worthy of worship. In Revelation, Jesus does not tell John to stop worshiping him. Knowing this feature of the apocalyptic genre helps us recognize one of the most important elements in the theology of Revelation: the worship of Jesus alongside God is appropriate. It is the genre of the book of Revelation that clues us in to this fact.

As you pursue the various genres of the Bible further, you will begin to see how genre might affect your perspective on any number of issues. To what extent, for example, were ancient biographies and histories exact in their presentations? Were authors permitted some license in the way they arranged and presented events? Should we even compare the Gospels or biblical histories to the ancient genres to which they come closest?

How does the standard format of an ancient letter shed light on the meaning of the letters in the New Testament? Are there pseudonymous writings in the Bible, written under the authority of key figures decades or even centuries after their deaths? Reading 2 Peter as a testament meant to convey the authority of Peter to a situation decades after his death will yield a different sense of its meaning than if you take it as a letter dictated by Peter himself in the late sixties of the first century.

Historical Context. The historical context is the historical background necessary to understand the original meaning of a book. As with the literary context, we can distinguish the immediate historical context or situation behind a book from its broader, historical background. The immediate situation behind the letter to Philemon is a slave trying to be reconciled to his master. Apparently, Onesimus did something that greatly offended his master, Philemon. As was often the case, Onesimus sought out a go-between: in this case, Paul. Paul writes Philemon urging him to forgive and receive Onesimus back, while offering to reimburse Philemon for any money Onesimus might have cost him.

Yet we can also speak of broader historical background. Ezra was written in the Persian period of Israel's history, several centuries after the Assyrians had destroyed the northern kingdom, and over a century after Babylon defeated the southern kingdom. It was written after the Babylonians destroyed the first temple and took its intelligentsia captive to Babylon. It was well over half a century after the Persians defeated the Babylonians and allowed the Jews to return to Jerusalem. It is against the backdrop of this broader historical background that Ezra comes to Jerusalem.

Knowing this background helps us interpret comments in various prophetic writings in the Old Testament. For example, some contemporary prophecy teachers use passages from the Old Testament to argue that modern Jews will one day rebuild a temple in modern-day Jerusalem. The problem is that the temple had already been rebuilt in 516 B.C., only to be destroyed again in A.D. 70. Ezekiel 40–43 was written before the second temple was rebuilt. And while that second temple was not as glorious as Ezekiel portrayed, it is not at all clear that Ezekiel's refer to some future temple yet to come.

There are other kinds of context too. There's the social setting of a writing, including, among other things, whether the author and audience were rich or poor, educated or illiterate. There are cultural matters like how marriage worked and whether people thought of themselves as individuals or formulated their identity in terms of the groups to which they belonged. Did they think in terms of honor and shame or individual guilt? All these factors affect the way we take the words of the Bible.

Take Jesus' answer to those who questioned him about paying taxes: "Give to Caesar what is Caesar's, and to God what is God's." We probably cannot understand what Jesus meant if we assume that money was as typical of Jesus' world as it is of ours. In rural Galilee, a village like Nazareth probably did not use coins very much. They likely did everything themselves, from making clothing to harvesting to making pots. The main reason they would need money was to pay taxes to someone or another—powers that were probably seen as oppressive in Jesus' day.

So Jesus was probably not saying that you should pay what you owe to Caesar and be a good citizen. Nor was Jesus dividing the world into distinct categories: things regarding citizenship or relating to religion. Rather, Jesus seems to dismiss Roman coinage itself as irrelevant to God. What did a follower of God in Palestine have to do with such things? Caesar is missing a coin? Give it back to him.

These are some of the dimensions that the question of context can take on. When we are trying to read the books of the Bible for their original meaning, we will need to consider these kinds of factors. The more we dig into context, the more we become aware of how differently these same words must have struck their original audiences from the way they tend to strike us. God may speak to us through the Bible's words out of context from time to time. But we will only gain in-depth understanding when we can also hear the words for what they actually meant when they were first inspired.

23

Many Books, Many Contexts

One of Martin Luther's principles in determining the meaning of the Bible was that "Scripture interprets Scripture." The problem with the way this principle is put into practice is that the biblical books were written by different authors who used words differently and wrote in three different languages. In such a situation, the way one author used words in one context cannot tell us how another author used words in another context.

We should weigh Scripture against Scripture, the meaning of one book against another. But you cannot usually interpret the original meaning of, say, Romans, by looking at the book of Matthew. Each author had his own vocabulary and way of putting things. If our understanding of inspiration does not account for the different meanings that words had in different contexts, then it is inadequate.

Let's look at an example. In Mark 8:12, Jesus says, "Why does this generation seek for a sign? Truly I say to you, [may I be accursed if a] sign will be given to this generation" (NASB). It is hard to find words in the English language that convey the Aramaic expression that lies behind this statement in Mark. To say the least, it strongly denies that Jesus was willing to provide a sign to the crowds.

Now consider John 20:30: "Jesus did many other miraculous signs in the presence of his disciples, which are not recorded in this book." What are some of the signs recorded in John? Turning water into wine for a public wedding was the first (John 2:11). John mentions that Jesus did several signs in Jerusalem (2:23) before a second miraculous sign (4:54). In short, John tells us that Jesus not only performed signs; he performed so many miraculous deeds that "if every one of them were written down, I suppose that even the whole world would not have room for the books that would be written" (John 21:25).

How do we fit these seemingly conflicting accounts together, if we should even try? Actually, while there might be some tension, these comments do not really contradict each other. Jesus clearly performed miraculous deeds in both Mark and John. The principal difference is that Mark and John use the word *sign* differently. John used it of any miraculous indication that Jesus is the Christ. Mark used it as a kind of proof on demand—like jumping through hoops at the behest of those who doubt. In the end, it is only when we take the individual vocabulary and perspectives of the two authors into account that we are saved from a rather significant contradiction here.

In terms of the original meaning, the literary context of an individual book extends only as far as that book itself. Revelation 22:18 says, "If anyone adds anything to [the words of the prophecy of this book], God will add to him the plagues described in this book," but it originally referred only to the book of Revelation rather than to the whole Bible. The books of the Bible were not placed in a single book at the time Revelation was written. At that time each book (or sometimes groups of smaller books) circulated on its own individual scroll.

It is not until the year A.D. 367 that we hear of someone even suggesting that the current list of books in our New Testament was the right list. Revelation was one of the books that early Christians debated over whether or not it was Scripture. It was not until the 300s that this debate became somewhat settled. Before then, godly Christians legitimately debated whether Revelation was as inspired as other books like Romans. This information is not meant to call into question the inspiration of Revelation, but to show that these books were originally written independently of each other, and thus, were meant to be read on their own terms—not in terms of each other.

The more we listen to each book, the more we will see the variety of the circumstances and perspectives in the Bible. You would not give the same advice to a serial killer and someone with a hyperactive conscience. In the same way, each book delivers a message appropriate to its circumstances and place in the flow of revelation. We probably listen best to the text when we see some of these books in dialogue with each other, even taking different sides on the same issues in a great debate.

For example, we mentioned earlier that Deuteronomy 24:1 freely allows a husband to divorce his wife if she becomes displeasing to him. In contrast, Malachi 2:14–16 speaks out against any man who might divorce the wife of his youth. Jesus will reinforce Malachi's complaint by forbidding men to divorce their wives for any old reason (Matt. 19:1–12). In this passage, Jesus considers the allowances of Deuteronomy contrary to God's original intention (19:8). So Jesus tells us that God made provisions in Scripture for something that was not his first preference.

Let us also consider books such as Joshua, where non-Israelites were obliterated regardless of their disposition to Israel or Yahweh (e.g., Josh. 6:21; 7:12; 9:24), and Ezra, where Israelites are commanded to divorce and send away their foreign wives and the children from such marriages (Ezra 10:3). These books seem to be in dialogue with books such as Jonah, where God freely forgives the atrocious Assyrians (e.g., Jon. 3:10), and Ruth, where a Moabitess is welcomed into the lineage of David (and thus Jesus; Ruth 4:18–22). The prophet Jonah seems to espouse a perspective similar to that of Joshua or Ezra—a perspective that the book of Jonah condemns.

Allowing the books of the Bible to speak on their own terms, rather than forcing them to fit together on our terms, presents us with a better understanding of the whole truth much more than if the books simply gave us a single voice. Reality is probably too complicated to be summed up in such a simple schema. Perhaps some truths are most accurately heard in the tension between what appears to be irreconcilable contradiction.

Beyond dialogue, we also observe a flow of revelation within and beyond the pages of the Bible. In Genesis, we soon realize that someone like Jacob (e.g., Gen. 31:34; 32:30) did not have nearly as good an understanding of God as Moses would (e.g., Ex. 6:3). Further, God presented the idea of monotheism more precisely in Isaiah (e.g., Isa. 44:6–20) than he did to Moses (Deut. 5:6–7; 32:8) or the psalmists (Ps. 82). When we get to the New Testament, we understand that Jesus must fit within God's divinity as Lord in some way (1 Cor. 8:6; Titus 2:13). We observe a clear development in understanding even within the pages of the Bible.

But even the New Testament did not resolve all these issues. Is Jesus to be worshiped in the same way we might bow our knee to a king (cf. Matt. 2:11)? What does 1 Corinthians 15:28 mean when it speaks of the ultimate subordination of Christ to God the Father? Does Hebrews 1:8–9 make a distinction between Christ as God and the God? Was the fourth century Arius interpreting Colossians correctly when he argued that the phrase "the firstborn over all creation" (Col. 1:15) meant Jesus was the first thing God created? Yet John 8:58 suggests that Jesus was the very same Yahweh who appeared to Moses at the burning bush. And the Lamb of Revelation 5:13 is worshiped alongside the One who sits on the throne.

Christians discussed these kinds of questions for four hundred years before such issues were finally settled. The church ultimately found that they had to resort to categories outside the Bible to resolve these issues. The Nicene Creed (A.D. 381), which gives the position Christians have taken on the Trinity ever since, includes a good dose of philosophical language that the early Christians used in order to make the necessary distinctions that we continue to use today.

We have reached a very important point in our exploration of hermeneutics. The individual books of the Bible were written independently of each other to address different contexts. Each book uses language and concepts in distinct ways. It logically follows that the task of connecting their teaching together and prioritizing them is an extra-biblical task. It is something we do as we look in on the Bible from the outside. The books of the Bible themselves do not tell us (for the most part) how their teaching might connect to the teaching of the other books.

Ezra and Joshua do not tell us how to relate their priorities to Jonah or Ruth. James does not tell us how to connect his "a person is justified *by what he does* and not by faith alone" (James 2:24) to Paul's "a man is justified by *faith* apart from observing the law" (Rom. 3:28) [emphasis mine]. An important step toward a mature use of Scripture is the acknowledgement that the glue that holds these concepts together in our thinking is not biblical glue—it ultimately cannot come from the Bible itself. Rather, it is glue that we bring from our personalities and backgrounds, not to mention the broader Christian traditions of which we are a part. This is not a bad thing—it becomes bad when we do not recognize it.

Such glue ideally will come from the Holy Spirit speaking through the church. But we note that the most important steps in the appropriation of the Bible for today are steps that the Bible itself cannot tell us how to take.

Bridging the Gap between That Time and This Time

Most of our discussion thus far has centered on the original meaning of the Bible. We have suggested that the pursuit of the original meaning is legitimate because it is, after all, the first meaning God inspired and produced the most formative moments in the tradition of the church. Yet it also provides depth and perspective in relation to any other meaning we might see in the words. At the same time, a number of important considerations make it clear that we should not base our beliefs and practices today solely on the original meaning of a biblical passage. In fact, the idea that we would get our beliefs and practices from Scripture alone is not possible, even given what we have learned thus far.

First of all, we should admit up front that in a vast number of cases, we simply do not have enough information to conclude what the original meaning of a passage was in the first place. Consider 2 Thessalonians 2:5, where Paul reminds the Thessalonians of a discussion he had with them while he was still at Thessalonica: "Don't you remember that when I was with you I used to tell you these things?" We would love to be privy to this information. But unfortunately, none of us are. Paul was not talking to us. We are not the "you" of this passage. Second Thessalonians 2 remains an extremely difficult passage to interpret because we have insufficient historical context to determine its meaning with certainty. Basing the Bible's authority strictly on the original meaning is problematic in part because we do not know for certain what Paul was referring to.

Even more problematic than the information that we know we lack, is the information we do not know we lack. In other words, new discoveries have repeatedly cast new light on old questions, revolutionizing the way we look at certain biblical texts. For example, the discovery of the Dead Sea Scrolls in 1947 continues to transform our understanding of various parts of the Bible today.

Further, with so many thousands of biblical scholars pouring over the text, the background literature, and the history of the Bible's interpretation, we are constantly hearing new perspectives on old questions. Occasionally, the waves of these discussions bring in new revolutions of insight—or at least trendy changes in interpretation. It is often difficult to know which trends will stand the test of time and which will pass quickly after they hit the shore. While the original meaning is a fairly stable meaning in theory, we cannot always identify it with certainty. We need some additional checks and balances in place as we try to appropriate it.

But even if we can know the original meaning with absolute certainty, a number of reasons exist for us not to assume that the original meaning will apply straightforwardly today. Whether in terms of belief or practice, a direct application of the words of the Bible to today can be inappropriate and even dangerous for several reasons.

POINT 1: Simply doing what the ancient audiences of the Bible's words did, would not be doing what they did if the significance, connotations, and implications are different today.

No one should assume that we are trying to get out of obeying the Bible with this observation. In many respects, working out the heart of biblical teaching today requires us to be more exacting than the Bible was originally. Jesus' interpretations of the Old Testament in Matthew 5 often fulfilled the Old Testament by exacting a more thorough standard than the Old Testament did. Yet it is equally clear that there are prohibitions and commands the Bible makes that would not make any sense in our context.

Take Paul's admonition to "greet all the brothers with a holy kiss" in 1 Thessalonians 5:26 or his urging of the women at Corinth to have a sign of authority on their head when they prophesy "because of the angels" (1 Cor. 11:10). Greeting my fellow brothers this way at my home church would not do what it did two thousand years ago—the connotations are now vastly different in twenty-first-century America.

And as to the 1 Corinthians 11:10 concern for a woman's sign of authority, scholars do not even agree on what Paul was talking about. I personally think Paul meant a woman should cover her head (not her face) with a veil when entering the spiritual presence of male beings like angels and God. So, consistent with her culture's mandates, the authority comes from the fact that she is honoring her "head"—her husband—as she is entering the presence of other men types (as it were). If this interpretation is correct, then you can see how foreign the logic of this passage is to us today (at least in our Western culture)—even among those who wear prayer bonnets or hair buns in lieu of this passage.

In other instances, we have to fulfill the heart of Scripture by a greater strictness than the Bible requires. Thus the Old Testament freely allows polygamy (e.g., Deut. 21:15–17). No passage ever complains about David or Solomon's many wives (except that they are foreign born). And it seems very unlikely that Ruth was Boaz's first wife. A wealthy, older man like him at that point in Israel's history probably had more than one wife before Ruth came into the picture.

The New Testament seems to assume that a person will have only one wife (e.g., 1 Cor. 7:2), but no passage in the New Testament explicitly prohibits polygamy for an ordinary person. First Timothy and Titus come the closest when they insist an overseer or deacon must be the husband of one wife (e.g., 1 Tim. 3:2, 12; Titus 1:6). These two books may mean something even stricter than monogamy—they may mean one wife during the course of a whole lifetime. Nevertheless, if we base our practices on the explicit teaching of the Bible alone, we have no prohibition of polygamy anywhere in the entire Bible.

However, in Western culture, polygamy seems incompatible with the very essence of Christianity. Some of the reasons we feel this way are probably based on misunderstandings of the social setting of the biblical text. For example, many Christians presume that polygamy is wrong because Genesis 2:24 speaks of a husband becoming one flesh with his wife. But it would be incorrect to think that this text originally meant you could only become one flesh with one person. No biblical text says such a thing. Jacob became one flesh with both his wives and his two concubines as well. And Paul speaks of becoming one flesh with a prostitute. There is no sense that one has thereby entered a marital or monogamous relationship with her (1 Cor. 6:16).

So on what basis is polygamy inappropriate for a Christian? I would suggest the main reason is that polygamy inevitably puts the wives into a less than ideal relationship with their husband. Polygamy implies a subordination and inequality of women to a man that will not be true of heaven. In that respect, it is only one step further away from the heavenly ideal than a marital relationship in which a single wife is subordinated to a single husband. Beyond this line of reasoning, it is hard to come up with any biblical argument against it on the basis of the original meaning. At this point we have a certain spiritual common sense that it is wrong, but might have difficulty arguing against it except that it does not seem fair or even-handed to the woman.

When the Sadducees tried to foil Jesus' understanding of resurrection, they presented him with a scenario in which a woman had become one flesh with seven brothers one after the other without having children (e.g., Mark 12:18–27). Whose wife would she then be in the kingdom? Jesus' answer was that there would not be marriage in the kingdom, and women would not be given to men (Mark 12:25). The subordination of wives to husbands will not exist in heaven, and all individuals of both genders will stand on an equal footing: "There is neither Jew nor Greek, slave nor free, male nor female, for you are all one in Christ Jesus" (Gal. 3:28).

It is possible that at various times and places on earth God has allowed his people to be polygamous. But such a practice is clearly less heavenly than monogamy. In the same way, God has, at times, allowed Christians to consider wives subordinate to their husbands (including in New Testament times). But this setup is less heavenly than marriages where both are on equal footing. As God allowed for divorce in the old covenant, perhaps God has winked at less than the ideal at various times and places (cf. Acts 17:30).

But in my view, Westerners today have no excuse to formulate the relationship between men and women on earth in these passing earthly terms—often based on certain misconceptions of the body. And we should urge Christians from polygamous cultures to move in a monogamous direction. When it comes to issues like these, God expects a higher standard today in the relationship between husbands and wives than he has sometimes allowed at other times and places.

POINT 2: God revealed the truths of the Bible within the paradigms and worldviews of the original audiences.

The point was not the ancient paradigm, but what God was affirming by way of it. We already mentioned that Paul says he was taken up into the "third heaven" in 2 Corinthians 12:2. The picture of three layers of heaven is just like what we find in the Testament of Levi, a Jewish writing of Paul's day. The writing takes you up through successive layers of heaven (or sky) until you get to where God is. So when Paul says that every knee will one day bow before Christ, he says it in the way he pictured the world: "of those in heaven, and those on earth, and those under the earth" (Phil. 2:10 NKJV). When Genesis conveys the creation of the stars, it sees them in the sky (Gen. 1:14) and it sees the sky as an expanse between the waters of the earth and certain primordial waters above the sky (Gen. 1:6).

When Colossians discusses the respectable relationships of the household (Col. 3:18—4:1), it does so in the same terms that Aristotle used in his *Politics*. Paul and Timothy discuss relationships of husband and wife, fathers and children, masters and slaves—the three domains that Aristotle lays out as the relationships of the household. When Paul speaks of the husband as the head of the wife and calls for her submission to the husband, he says the same thing that Aristotle did.

My point here is not to dismiss these passages (which I affirm as inspired for their original audiences). But we need to see that it is important to clarify what the point of these passages was and what it was not. Paul's point in Philippians was not the structure of the cosmos, but the ultimate submission of the world to Christ. And Genesis 1 no doubt showed who God was in contrast to the gods of pagan creation stories—more than giving us a slide show of the creation process.

And the point of the household codes of Colossians, Ephesians, and 1 Peter probably has more to do with being a good witness to non-Christians than God's timeless plan for the household. First Peter prefaces its household instructions with the general principle that Christians should "live such good lives among the pagans that, though they accuse you of doing wrong, they may see your good deeds and glorify God on the day he visits us" (1 Pet. 2:12). Ironically, to fulfill the purpose of this verse, we would need to allow wives to have equal value and freedom in our households today. We would be a bad witness to our world if we were to force our wives to be subordinate to their husbands simply because of their gender, never mind trying to practice the submission of slaves to masters in a household.

Because the inspired message of the Bible's books came in the clothing of ancient paradigms and worldviews, much discernment is necessary when appropriating the biblical text for today. Thus the Bible was not meant to tell us about how the brain works. Various parts of the Bible conceptualize the human make-up differently (e.g., Genesis uses the soul of a whole living person; Hebrews thinks of the soul as part of a person). The process of appropriating the original meaning of the Bible will require us to discern what the inspired point of each passage was, as well as the ancient clothing in which it was dressed.

POINT 3: In some cases, the people of the New Testament had not yet reached a final answer on certain beliefs and practices.

We have already mentioned the matter of polygamy. Add slavery to that list. It is highly doubtful that Paul was asking Philemon to give Onesimus his emancipation from slavery in the book of Philemon. The text never says anything like this. Colossians, which Paul may have sent to the same destination at the same time, instructs slaves to obey their earthly masters and says not a word to masters about setting their slaves free (Col. 3:22—4:1).

The New Testament does not spell out the specifics of the Trinity or exactly what the divinity of Christ is. God worked out these understandings in the church through the centuries that followed. Actually, there are several issues on which the books of the New Testament have yet to reach a final answer. Take the issue of earthly sacrifice. According to Acts 21, Paul goes to the temple to offer animal sacrifices to release certain individuals from a vow (21:26). But Hebrews tells of the end of all animal sacrifice in the light of Christ's once and for all atonement (Heb. 10:14).

In the years that have followed the New Testament, God has made it immensely clear to us that an earthly temple is not only unnecessary; it would be blasphemous in the light of Christ's once and for all sacrifice. But it is not clear that all the New Testament authors had fully come to understand this fact yet. It is at least possible that when 1 Timothy 2:15 speaks of women being saved from transgression through childbearing, it still reflects the kind of old covenant thinking. In retrospect we know that the book of Hebrews gives the final answer.

This example is particularly instructive. In the books of the New Testament alone, you could, in theory, give greater priority to those parts that say nothing about animal sacrifice in the Jerusalem temple. In theory, you could take Hebrews 10:8 and argue that animal sacrifices are still part of this age, which is near disappearance, but has not yet disappeared completely. Why is it that Christians do not prioritize and synthesize the New Testament teaching in this way? We do not process the teaching of the New Testament in this way because God has made it very clear in the history of the church that Hebrews gives the final answer on this issue.

POINT 4: These books do not tell us how to connect their teaching to each other.

We already mentioned this fact in the preceding section. The activity of creating a biblical theology—determining the general thrust of the Bible on a particular topic or issue—is a matter of us looking in from the outside. It is an extra-biblical task. The Bible itself does not tell us how to fit these books together. And the more their language and imagery is in tension with each other, the more we have to do with what we understand the biblical teaching on that topic to be.

Take the matter of women and spiritual leadership in the church. We cannot simply consider 1 Timothy 2:12 to be the biblical teaching on the subject: "I do not permit a woman to teach or to have authority over a man." We must connect this particular passage in 1 Timothy with all the other biblical teaching relating to women on this subject. Thus we will also need to consider the implications of Acts 18:26: "When Priscilla and Aquila heard him [Apollos], *they* invited him to *their* home and explained to him the way of God more adequately" (emphasis mine). We will need to consider the prophetic role that Acts 2:17–18 and 1 Corinthians 11:5 present for women. To be careful, we should not apply any one of these individual passages directly to today until we have considered all the others.

POINT 5: They do not tell us how their teaching might connect to our time.

Not only do we need to connect the individual teachings of the Bible's books to each other, we are also need to figure out how to apply their original meaning to our quite different contexts. Since the books were written to the ancient audiences, the Bible does not tell us how these words might relate to us—how to connect their world to our world. Determining this connection is an extra-biblical task.

So to return to the question of women in roles of spiritual leadership, we first look at the teaching of each book of the Bible on the subject. We find one instance where women are said not to teach men for various reasons (1 Tim. 2:12). Yet we find a number of instances where women do teach men (Acts 19:26), take roles of leadership (Judg. 4:4; Rom. 16:1, 7), and prophesy as part of the age of the Spirit's arrival (1 Cor. 11:5; Acts 2:17–18). In 2 Kings 22:14, the person with the greatest spiritual knowledge in all Israel was the prophetess Huldah. Even the high priest went to her for the most important spiritual decision Israel needed to make in several hundred years.

We might sum up the biblical landscape on this topic by saying that while most spiritual leadership in the Bible is provided by men, there are also clear instances where women perform the same spiritual functions. The prophecy of Acts 2:17–18 leads us to believe that women will increasingly take on such roles in this age in which we live. This is the age of the Holy Spirit, and both men and women equally have the Spirit. In Christ there are no longer male and female hierarchies (Gal. 3:28).

We've already seen that the entire process of connecting biblical teaching together takes place outside the biblical text. It is something we do; the Bible does not do it for us. It is the same with connecting the worlds of the biblical books with our world. Is there anything about our time that will move us closer to women taking on roles of spiritual leadership? Further away from it? The answer we provide is again one that the Bible does not tell us. We have to discern it spiritually.

The more we recognize how much weight is placed on us in interpretation, the more we will humbly plead for the Spirit's help. We will want to seek out the body of Christ to read and apply Scripture together. If the Spirit of Christ inhabits the body of Christ, then we are more likely to hear God's voice authentically when we are in communion with the saints of the ages, and not just lone ranger interpreters.

With regard to women, I would take a prophetic stance. Today our social setting would not lead us to restrict the roles of women in order to be a good witness to our world. Instead, we are a bad witness to our world if we put artificial barriers around them, in contrast to the world in which 1 Peter 2:12 was written. Unlike the ancient world, we do not live in a culture where women are less educated or more easily deceived than men. Actually, the tremendous gains we have made in our understanding of the brain tell us that there is no physical basis for making these kinds of distinctions. And we know what heaven will be like (Mark 12:25; Gal. 3:28). I submit that in our world today, to subordinate women to men or to refuse them any role in the church to which God is calling them is to work against the direction in which God is moving.

So once we construct a biblical theology on a particular topic, we must consider the relationship between the biblical world and our world. We find points of continuity and discontinuity between the two, and identify the flow of revelation in the church. Only then can we be certain that we are today carrying out the teaching of the original meaning with God's blessing. If we do not allow for some process of this sort, we may just find ourselves like the religious leaders who opposed Jesus, or the Judaizers who opposed Paul. In that day, they were the literalists and absolutists. Jesus and Paul were the ones who interpreted Scripture spiritually rather than by the letter.

POINT 6: The New Testament does not directly address many of the issues that are most pressing for our time.

It is common to assume that the Bible gives us all the answers we need for our questions today. Unfortunately, the Bible does not address some of the issues on which we most desire a word from God. Although the concept of abortion existed at the time of the New Testament, the New Testament does not address the subject. Any verses we might discover on the topic are indirectly relevant at best. And where will we find verses on stem cell research or removing feeding tubes from people who are brain dead?

We will not find passages that directly address many of the current issues on which we most want a word from God. The verses brought to bear on these subjects are often those most read out of context. This is not a point of despair. It is a reminder for the church to pray and take the responsibility that it has always had. Protestants in particular have overreacted to the excesses of the medieval Roman Catholic church and have not wanted to acknowledge these responsibilities. It is easier to pretend that there is a quick answer in a verse taken out of context than to go through the process of "working out [our] salvation with fear and trembling" (Phil. 2:12). God did not stop speaking when he inspired the books of the Bible. It is the church's job to listen to what he is saying today.

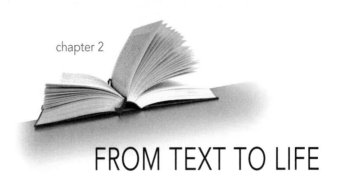

chapter 2

FROM TEXT TO LIFE

AN OVERVIEW FROM TEXT TO LIFE

In the next few pages we want to run through the typical process by which someone might move from text to life. In general, there are two players in this process: the text and the reader. Some speak of these two as the two horizons of the text.

In the section on hermeneutics, we saw that the original world of the text was an ancient world. While God is not limited to the world of the original meaning, we must respect the original meaning. We wouldn't like it if someone listening to us completely ignored what we were trying to say. Christian love at least respects the world of the original text, even if it is not limited to it.

So we have a two step text-to-life process: (1) determine as much as possible the original meaning; and (2) determine as much as possible the relationship between that meaning and us.

Here is an overview of what such a process might look like.

Pray!

It is bad theology to think that prayer doesn't apply to studying Scripture. Our minds are too fallible in our reasoning. In addition, there are many points where we simply do not have enough information to know the original meaning or how it relates to us today. We need the Spirit's guidance through these moments of uncertainty. By all means, pray before you begin the process of moving from text to life.

Determine What the Original Text Said

We do not have an original copy of any of the books of the Bible. We have very early ones—especially compared to the works of other ancient writers like Plato or Caesar. But there is enough difference in the wording of these ancient copies of the various books that we are still forced to make decisions about the way the original texts might have read.

This is why the King James Version (KJV) sometimes has different words than other English versions. If you try to look up Acts 8:37 in most modern versions, you'll find it isn't included in the main text. The man who divided the Bible into verses in the 1500s was using the same basic manuscripts that the KJV was based on, so he assigned a verse number to Acts 8:37. But since then, we have found copies of the New Testament that are much older than the

ones used by the KJV translators in 1611. The vast majority
of those who have studied this issue agree that the relatively
late medieval copies of the Bible that the KJV was based on
were not as accurate to the original texts as those that stand
behind almost all other English translations today.

We can debate whether we really need to determine the
original wording to hear God in Scripture. If you're aiming
to discover the original meaning, however, you will want to
take *textual criticism*—the science of determining the original wording—into account. This book will not describe
the process of how to decide what the original text of a passage might have said. But you should be aware of this step
in the process, one that you will have to let someone else
do for you if you choose not to learn the skill. We should
be immensely thankful to the many scholars who have
devoted their whole lives to determining the likely way
the original text read.

Observation: What Does the Text Say?

Whether you are moving from text to life or life to
text, you will want to learn the skill of observation—the
ability to distinguish between what the text says and what
it doesn't say. Probably well over half the issues Christian
groups debate about today have to do with things the Bible
doesn't even say. The person who is asking the kinds of
questions that the text wants to answer is the person who
is accurately observing what the text says. These may not

be the questions we want to ask or the questions we need answered, but they are the questions that the text originally asked and answered.

There are two different modes of observation. One aims at the big picture of a book, a section of a book, or a passage. This mode of observation sees where one thought ends and another begins, and how they relate to each other. A second mode aims to observe the fine details of a verse or smaller passage. You will almost certainly need to be aware of the original Hebrew, Aramaic, or Greek for your detailed observations to be precise in relation to the original meaning. We will briefly discuss both these modes of observation in the next section.

Interpretation: What Did the Text Mean?

If good observation skills raise the kinds of questions the text wants to answer, good interpretation skills come up with the most likely answers to those questions. In the section on hermeneutics, we saw that context determines the meaning of words. Good interpretation of the original meaning will correctly place the text you are interpreting in the right context.

We've already mentioned some of the key contexts to take into consideration. There's the immediate literary context of the text you are looking at. Given the train of thought that leads up to the words you are trying to interpret, you must ask yourself what those words mean. Then there is the broader literary context. Given what the author says in similar contexts in this same book, what are these words likely to mean here? The context of genre is a larger literary context that can have a significant effect on how you understand certain words. The historical context places the words in question against a broader historical background, including other books by the same author.

Another key tool in interpretation is word and phrase study. Many preachers and interpreters have a magical view of word meanings that, while it makes for interesting preaching, isn't quite accurate to the way words actually work. A whole previous generation of scholars also labored under a number of fallacious ways of using word studies. These slight misunderstandings have not prevented God from speaking to be sure! But we will briefly examine some fallacies to beware of in our section on interpretation.

Integration: Mapping the Texts to Each Other

Our section on hermeneutics mentioned that the individual books of the Bible do not connect their individual teachings to one another. We must do that from the outside looking in. Joining these teachings together, mapping one part of the Bible to another, is a theological task. When we say that "the Bible says" or "the biblical worldview says," we are usually referring to a biblical theology that we have created by gluing the parts of Scripture together.

It is crucial to recognize that we are the ones who provide this glue because the Bible, "Scripture alone," does not provide it for us.

Sometimes the glue we use to connect the individual materials of the Bible together can be much like the biblical material itself. Paul tells us how to glue the Old Testament teaching on the Sabbath to his teaching. When we recognize that he was writing to Gentiles, and Matthew was likely writing to Jewish Christians, we can map their teaching on the law in a way that is directly applicable to what we are doing—all while still retaining the meaning that is fairly close to the biblical world.

At other times, though, we must insert ourselves—and the subsequent history of Christianity—much more into this integration process. For example, understanding the biblical teaching on women in ministry calls for a more sophisticated approach than many other issues. The reason is that we receive mixed signals from the Old Testament and the New Testament. As we attempt to integrate the teaching within the Bible and connect it to our world, we can easily blur the task of integration into the task of appropriation simply because we know more of where the flow of revelation and the new covenant were leading than many of the biblical writers did. Avoiding this trap requires great diligence on the part of the interpreter.

Appropriation: Applying the Text to Life

If one is moving strictly from text to life, the final step is the appropriation of the biblical text to life. If you believe you have found the center of biblical teaching on an issue, making the jump to today can involve any number of considerations. For example, you may want to look at points of continuity and discontinuity between a specific passage you are looking at and our world today—how is our situation alike and different? You will want to locate that passage within the flow of biblical revelation—where does it fall in relation to Christ and the new covenant? You will also want to consider how the Christians of the ages have dealt with that passage or issue. If virtually all Christians have taken a particular position on an issue throughout the centuries, that seems significant! Listen to the Holy Spirit, use spiritual common sense, and then make the jump from text to life.

In the rest of this section, we'll go into greater depth on two of these skills: observation and interpretation. Then in the final section, we will explore integration and appropriation in greater depth.

OBSERVATION

The skill of observation is the ability to notice what the text says (and thus by implication, what it does not say). In our introduction to the text-to-life process, we mentioned that there are two levels of skill for observing the biblical text. They are: observing the big picture of a book or section and observing the details of a text.

Surveying a Text

To see the big picture of a biblical text, you need to do three things. First, determine where one line of thought ends and another begins throughout the book or section you are surveying. Second, describe the way each major thought flows into the next. Finally, identify the themes that run throughout the book or section of the book.

The first skill amounts to outlining the book (or section of the book). Can you observe places where the author is moving on to a new thought? For example, Romans 12:1 says, "Therefore, I urge you, brothers [and sisters], to offer your bodies as living sacrifices. . . ." This indicates that Paul is now moving on to a new section of Romans and new train of thought. In terms of the big picture, we are talking about big blocks of thought. Romans 1:18—11:36 seems to be one big unit of thought. And Romans 12:1

Introduction 1:1–15	Body of the Letter to the Romans 1:16—15:13		Closing Remarks 15:14–33	Recommendation Letter 16:1–24
	The Right-eousness of God Revealed in the Gospel 1:16—11:36	Transformed Minds and Bodies 12:1—15:13		

through 15:13 is another big block of thought. A good observer of Romans should be able to break down its overall argument into big blocks of thought, which can then be broken down even further (see the chart).

The second skill in surveying is to see how big blocks of text connect to each other. We have observed that Romans 12:1 starts a new section of Romans. A skillful observer tries to understand how the first and second major parts of Romans fit together, and finds a cause and effect relationship. Because of what Paul has taught in the first half, "therefore," the second half follows.

Here are some of the main ways that two blocks of thought can flow from one to the other:

1. The first block can *prepare* or lay the background for what follows in a very general way. For example, the birth stories in Matthew and Luke prepare for what follows. If you prefer, you can call this pattern the introduction.
2. The two blocks of thought can *compare* or *contrast*. The alternating stories of David and Saul tend to contrast with each other.
3. The first unit can be *general* and the second go into the *particulars* or details. Or, it can go the other way around: the first unit can be the particulars and the second generalizes what has gone before. So if a book of the Bible has key verses, they

can be a general statement that the remainder of the book plays out (like Acts 1:8).

4. The first can lead to the second in a number of different ways. It can be a fairly straightforward cause that leads to an effect. After Pentecost, all sorts of miracles and boldness start to happen. But ideas can follow from other ideas in an argument as well in a kind of *logical causation*. In Romans, the practical preaching of Romans 12–15 follows from the more theoretical teaching of Romans 1–11. A *conclusion* is also a kind of effect caused by what has preceded it.

5. Some specialized cause and effect patterns are the movement from *problem to solution* or from *question to answer*. Much of Romans is structured as questions and answers.

Themes can also run throughout a book or part of a book. A good observer can thus see *recurrences*. In Philippians, rejoicing and unity are recurring themes. The kinds of patterns we mentioned above can also recur. Hebrews is full of recurring contrasts between Christ and various figures from the Old Testament.

So given the outline of Romans on the previous page, we might ask how each of the big blocks of material relate to each other. For example, how do the introductory paragraphs of Romans relate to the rest of the letter? Certainly they prepare or set the background for what follows. But if we look carefully, we might also notice that Romans 1:16–17 gives us a kind of general statement that Paul unfolds over the next eleven chapters. In other words, the argument of Romans is structured in a movement from general to particular.

We have already mentioned that the first main part of the argument of Romans (1:16 — 11:36) leads logically to the second part (12:1 — 15:13). So Romans is structured by a logical movement of cause to effect. The closing remarks of Romans clearly constitute a conclusion for the letter.

After looking at how the big sections of Romans relate to each other, we should read through Romans to look for recurring themes. Some of these will fit with the fact that 1:16–17 unfolds throughout the rest of the book. Themes like the gospel, salvation, God's righteousness, and justification by faith recur throughout Romans. We have already said as much when we said that Romans 1:16–17 is a general statement that plays out in the particulars that follow.

But we might find some other themes that recur. For example, the idea that sin leads to death and condemnation, while faith leads to life and justification, is a theme that recurs throughout the bulk of the letter. Similarly, we find a comparison throughout the letter between Jews and Gentiles — justification takes place the same for both in exactly the same way (we might actually consider this theme part of the general to particular pattern based on Romans 1:16–17, since Paul mentions Jew and Gentile there). I find it helpful to go through the list of patterns above and ask if I can find any instances of cause and effect, general to particular, and other patterns, that are significant enough to include in an overview or survey.

Once you have surveyed a portion of text, you will probably have questions that you want to address when you get deeper into interpretation. Before you move on, there are two final things to do after you have outlined and analyzed the patterns and themes of a text. The first is to identify important verses and passages in the overall meaning of the text you are surveying. I had a seminary professor who called these "strategic areas." In our survey of Romans, we saw in chapter 1 that verses 16–17 were very important verses to understand so that we can grasp what the book as a whole is about. You might write those verses down so you can come back and explore them in more detail later.

A second thing to do is to write down the *questions* you think will best unlock the secrets of what you have surveyed. If you have done a good job of finding the key patterns and themes of a book or section, then those are the kinds of things you most want to ask questions about in interpretation. If you understand the key patterns and themes of a particular text inside and out, then you have understood what it is really about.

Here are the kinds of questions you might ask: questions of *definition, who* questions, *where* questions, *when* questions, *how* questions, *why* questions, and questions about the *implications*. Be careful with questions of implication, because at this point we are still trying to figure out what the text *meant*, not what it means for us today. When we are trying to figure out the original meaning, an implication refers to what the implications were for the original author and audience.

To summarize, we can survey a whole book of the Bible or a smaller block within a book by following these steps:

1. Get a sense of the content of the book or section. You might read through it in one sitting two or three times (admittedly, this gets harder the bigger the book—but you would be amazed at how much you gain from a skim through Isaiah). You might give a title to each chapter just to get a sense of what's there.
2. Outline the book or section. Be sure to look for big blocks of thought, not just ten smaller ones.
3. Observe how these big sections connect with each other.
4. Observe themes or patterns running through the whole book or section.
5. Identify verses or passages that are key to the overall plan and meaning of the text.
6. Ask questions about the patterns and themes you have identified. These questions will lead into good interpretation.

Now you have a method by which you can get the overall picture of a larger amount of biblical text.

Observing in Detail

If you really want to hone in on the meaning of a verse or a small amount of text, you will need to develop your skills at observing the details of the text. It is very difficult to do this with an English translation (or a translation into any other language) because the details of a translation will rarely capture all the details of the original language. I once heard a pastor make a point from the word *at* in the King James Version of Titus 2:5, which speaks of young women being "keepers *at* home." But this whole phrase comes entirely from one Greek word—there is no Greek word for *at* in the original text.

So the best you can do for detailed observation in English is to get a good formal equivalence translation. These are versions like the New American Standard Version, the Revised Standard Version, or the English Standard Version. The New King James Version is also a good formal equivalence translation, especially if you know the places where it differs from the original.

There are different ways to help your mind observe the details of a passage. I find a lot of people like to write down or photocopy some verses and then write all over it the various things they notice. They draw all kinds of circles, squares, underlines, and so forth, with lines leading to comments they write all around the page. I usually ask them then to make two columns on the back of the page and to put their most interesting observations on one side and any questions those observations raise on the other side. You can then follow up on those questions in interpretation.

A more thorough way to observe a text is to make two columns. Put the text on one side and your observations on the other. You might first make observations about how one sentence connects to the next, then how each clause within a sentence relates to any other clauses within the sentence, then how each word and phrase relates to other elements of the clause. You might even have a third column for crucial questions that you can come back to during interpretation. You can see a sample of what this might look like for a small portion of Romans 1:16 by looking at the following chart.

It might help to go through the following list of things to observe. First, look for the key terms and phrases. These raise important questions of definition that can lead to important word studies. Second, look for key grammatical features like tenses of verbs or singular and plural.

Next, look for the way words connect to each other (syntax). Aside from the main point of a sentence, you often find subordinate clauses that express things like purpose, conditions, timing, and so forth. Fourth, look for the same kinds of logical connections we mentioned under surveying (cause-effect, general to particular, etc.). Finally,

Text	Observation	Questions
"the gospel"	This is what Paul is not ashamed of.	• What is the gospel? • Why is Paul not ashamed of the gospel? • How does Paul's not being ashamed show itself in the way he relates to the Romans?
"for"	"For" is a conjunction that usually either explains or substantiates what has just been said. Here Paul is about to explain why he is not ashamed of the gospel.	• How does the fact that the gospel is the power of God to salvation explain why Paul is not ashamed of it?
"it is the power of God for salvation"	The gospel is the power of God.	• What is the power of God? • How is the gospel the power of God? • Why is the gospel the power of God?
	It is . . . for salvation.	• What is salvation? • What does it mean for the power of God to lead to salvation? • How does the power of God lead to salvation? • Why does the power of God lead to salvation? • What are the implications for the Romans given that the power of God leads to salvation?

there are other miscellaneous features to look for, like tone, figurative expressions, interaction with other texts, varying points of view, and items of historical background.

Sometimes the text of the Bible becomes so familiar to us that we miss obvious but significant details. One of the benefits of training yourself to observe everything about the text is that you will see these sorts of obvious things. This is also one of the benefits of reading the Bible in its original Greek, Hebrew, or Aramaic. Reading in a foreign language forces you to slow down and pay attention to the details in a way you might not otherwise do. Suddenly you stop to observe the word *but* and immediately recognize that something is being contrasted with something else. You observe important connecting words like *therefore*, *for*, and *because*. You observe the relationships between thoughts that we mentioned above (cause-effect, general-particular, contrast).

INTERPRETATION

Good observation skills move you down the road toward good interpretation. In the methods of observation we presented above, we suggested you write down questions that you can directly focus on during interpretation. You have tried to observe what the text says. Now you want to know what it meant. In reality, these two movements take place simultaneously and are hard to separate from one another. When you observe that the thought of Romans 1–11 leads to the thought of Romans 12–15, you have not only observed something, you have begun to interpret Romans. Regardless of whether you are interpreting the text from text to life or life to text, you will want to have the skills of observation and interpretation at the table with you to give their voice.

We saw in the hermeneutics section that words only take on definite meanings in a context. So the process of interpretation is the process of finding the right context against which to read the various words of the Bible. In this section, we are going to focus on determining the original meaning of biblical texts. Because these were the first meanings these texts had, they deserve our respect. We are returning to the various contexts we mentioned in the hermeneutics section to see, in more detail, how they affect our interpretations. In life, of course, these may not be the most important meanings of the text for us. God may meet you in these words in a way that places them in your context with a divine urgency. We will say more about the context of our horizon in the next section.

The Immediate Context

The most determining context of all for the original meaning is the immediate literary context of the words you are looking at. We have already discussed this in the hermeneutics section. A word, or a set of words, can mean many things both literally and metaphorically. All words have a certain range of possible meanings that they can take on. They do not mean all these things at once. A specific context locks on to one of these (less often a text can also have a double entendre, a double meaning).

One common fallacy among Bible students is to take the specific meaning a word or phrase has in one context and read them into another. So if the phrase *cast out* is used in relation to demons in a passage of Mark, they might read spiritual warfare into another place where the same word is used. You can't do this—not if you are aiming for the original meaning. *Casting out* will only have overtones of demons if the passage you are looking at uses the word in that way! This is a form of what is called the *overload fallacy*—putting more meaning into a word than it should have at any given time. It usually happens when a person brings too much baggage with them from one place where a word is used to the next.

This type of mistake is made so often that it is worth another paragraph. Take the word *faith*. Its basic meaning on any one occasion is pretty narrow. In Greek, the word *pistis* can mean many different things: trust, belief, faithfulness, proof, and so forth. But it does not mean all these at the same time. And more importantly, it does not always mean "trust in the unseen" just because it has this specific connotation in Hebrews 11:1.

This is perhaps the most common error made when studying the original meaning of a word—taking the very specific meanings a word has in one context and then stuffing those connotations into a completely different context. "Will their lack of faith nullify God's faithfulness?" (Rom. 3:3). The word *faith* in this verse had nothing to do with justification by faith or faith in the unseen. In its immediate context, it simply meant the faithfulness of God.

Getting a sense of the immediate context of a word or passage requires us to follow the train of thought leading up to it. This involves the skill of detailed observation we mentioned in the previous section—being able to observe how one thought leads to the next. Romans 11:26 gives us a good example of paying attention to the immediate context of a verse. On the one hand, many students of Romans notice that Paul somewhat redefines Israel in Romans 9:6: "not all who are descended from Israel are Israel." When Paul later says in Romans 11:26 that "all Israel will be saved," some think he does not mean the Jews, but all who belong to the true Israel: the Christians.

But while this reading pays good attention to the broader context of the verse, it does not pay as good attention to the immediate context of Romans 11:26. The verse previous to 11:26 clearly uses Israel in reference to ethnic Jews—"Israel has experienced a hardening." The immediate train of thought in 11:25 thus pushes us to take "all Israel" in 11:26 as a reference to that ethnic Israel whose hearts were hardened in Paul's day, not to the redefined Israel of Romans 9:6.

As a method, you might begin the interpretation of a specific passage first with a detailed observation of it, and then with a preliminary glance at the immediate context to brainstorm. You might then move out through the following contexts, revising and revisiting your initial brainstorm. By the time you have considered all the various contexts of the passage, you will be ready to draw a more definite conclusion on what it meant originally in its immediate context.

Broader Literary Context

We have already mentioned broader literary context. Broader literary context is the rest of the section in which a passage appears, as well as the book as a whole. In the case of Romans 11:26 above, Romans 9–11 and the book of Romans as a whole are part of the broader literary context of that verse.

Other books by the same author can also help us see how an author tended to use a particular word, although technically such writings are part of the historical rather than literary context. We must be careful because even individual authors can change the way they use words over time. In the case of Paul's writings, for example, the thought and use of words is different enough in some of the letters that scholars actually debate whether Paul himself crafted the words of some of them (e.g., 1 Tim. and Titus).

Along the same lines, different authors in the Old and New Testament used various words and concepts differently from each other. The Old and New Testament are even in different languages, so you certainly can't assume that an English word from a translation of the Old Testament will have the same meaning as an English word from a translation of the New Testament. These books can constitute historical background for each other, but in terms of their original meaning, they should not be treated as part of the same book. The Bible was originally a library rather than a single text.

This might be a good place to mention another mistake people sometimes make in interpretation: the *anachronistic fallacy*. The anachronistic fallacy is when you mistake a meaning a word took on later in the history of a language (or even later in history) and read it back into a time when it didn't exist. Although the Greek word for *witness* is *martyr*, it didn't take on the sense of a martyr as we know it today until after the New Testament was written. Similarly, the Hebrew word for *soul* never had the sense of a part of me that detaches at death. A soul in Hebrew is always alive (as opposed to a part of a person that survives death). It referred to an entire living creature—even a living sea creature! "[Adam] became a living soul" (Gen. 2:7 KJV).

Isaiah 9 gives another helpful case study in how the broader context can potentially illuminate the likely original meaning of a passage. When we read the amazing comments in Isaiah 9:6, it is extremely difficult for us not to hear a reference to Jesus: "to us a child is born, to us a son is given. . . . He will be called 'Wonderful Counselor,' 'Mighty God' . . ." What other human could someone call

God? Despite the context we are about to discuss, this passage, like others in Isaiah, seems to move beyond the first context. No matter what the first meaning, we are not wrong to read this passage in the light of Jesus. After all, that is the way the Holy Spirit has long led Christians to read this passage throughout history.

But a look at the broader context of Isaiah 9 takes us back to a similar passage in Isaiah 7: "The virgin shall conceive and bear a Son, and shall call His name Immanuel" (7:14 NKJV). In the immediate context of that verse, a king named Ahaz is considering making an alliance with a foreign nation. Isaiah, representing God, does not want him to do so. God offers Ahaz a sign of his favor. But Ahaz will have nothing to do with it.

It is in this immediate context that the well known words of Isaiah 7:14 appear. Isaiah basically says, "Okay, if you're not going to ask for a sign, then the Lord himself will give you a sign. A child will be born, and before that child is old enough to tell the difference between good and evil, the nations to the north that are bothering you will be gone."

In the original context, the sign is clearly for Ahaz. That makes it highly unlikely that Jesus was the child Isaiah himself had in mind. After all, Jesus was born over seven hundred years later. A sign that comes that long after Ahaz is dead is hardly a sign to him! So the Immanuel whom Isaiah originally referred to was probably some child born very soon after he and Ahaz had this conversation. Thus, this human child represented "God with us."

Again, the Holy Spirit inspired Matthew to see Jesus' virgin birth in the words of Isaiah 7:14. God placed those words against the context of Jesus and they took on new meanings for Matthew. But originally, the sign was a human child born in the days of Ahaz. This child was perhaps one of Ahaz's own children.

When we consider this broader context to Isaiah 9, we naturally wonder if Isaiah 9:6 is referring to the same royal child as 7:14, perhaps even king Hezekiah who was Ahaz's son: "Wonderful Counselor, Mighty God, Everlasting Father, Prince of Peace." That doesn't mean that God can't apply the words literally to Jesus as well in our context, with a different connotation. But the broader context of Isaiah suggests we should probably see the original meaning in terms of some ancient royal figure like Hezekiah. Psalm 45:6 shows that in poetic language, Scripture could use exaggerated language and refer to the earthly king as God since he was God's representative on earth (cf. Ps. 45:7 and 12–16).

Historical Context

The historical context of Isaiah also pushes us in this direction. Once again, by historical context we mean the background of these words in history, within which we should include all the events and all the other writings of the day. In our discussion of the literary context of Isaiah 7–9, we mentioned a number of elements in its historical background: king Ahaz, the kings to the north who were troubling him, his son and heir Hezekiah. If we were to interpret this passage in greater detail we would want to mention the king of Assyria and the destruction of the kingdom just to the north of Ahaz in 722–21 B.C.

But also in the cultural background is the fact that various cultures in the ancient Near East, including Israelite culture, referred to their kings as gods. For Israel, of course, calling the king "god" did not in any way mean that he was a God like Yahweh. We mentioned Psalm 45 earlier. In its context it refers to a human king on his wedding day. Look at verses 6–7 where the psalmist refers to the king as god: "Your throne, O god, is forever and ever . . ." But the next verse makes it clear that this king is not the ultimate God: "therefore God, *your* God . . ." [emphasis mine]. So the Old Testament refers to human kings both as sons of God (e.g., 2 Sam. 7:14) and even as god in a somewhat figurative sense.

Acquiring historical background knowledge is a lifetime task. And unfortunately, even if you knew everything there was to know, you would still have such vastly incomplete knowledge of the ancient world that you would not be able to know with certainty what every part of the Bible meant. Our attempts to interpret Isaiah and Paul above are only informed attempts. Various scholars would disagree on various points, and any day a new discovery might force us to rethink everything.

The best place to get background knowledge is a good original meaning commentary on the passage you are interpreting. In theory, the scholar who has written the commentary has done his or her homework and will inform you of various background information that you would not otherwise have known. Numerous Bible dictionaries and books on the culture of the ancient world are also available to help you fill in this part of the puzzle.

Genre

The section on hermeneutics above has already mentioned the matter of genre and how it can affect your interpretation of a particular passage. We will not repeat what we have already covered there. Suffice it to say that genre is yet another type of literary context that can direct the meaning of a passage in a particular direction.

Doing Word and Phrase Studies

A word or phrase study is an investigation that aims to figure out what a particular word or phrase means. It is really a microcosm of the whole interpretive process. The process of doing a word study might look like this:

1. Get a basic definition for the Hebrew, Aramaic, or Greek word from an original meaning dictionary of some sort. Don't use an English dictionary. Words don't map from one language to another exactly. An English dictionary tells you how words are being used *right now* in English. You

need to know how a Greek, Hebrew, or Aramaic word was being used at the time an ancient author used it.

If you don't have an original meaning dictionary, blueletterbible.org is a good resource to find out the original word behind the English and a starting definition. Don't rely too heavily on the dictionaries at this Website. They are prone to the overload fallacy we mentioned above.

If you have a *Strong's Exhaustive Concordance of the Bible*, you can look up the English word and follow the number beside it to where the Greek, Hebrew, and Aramaic word behind it is listed. It will give you enough of a definition to start your study.

Some other resources that can clue you in to the original words are *Young's Analytical Concordance to the Bible*, *Englishman's Hebrew Concordance of the Old Testament*, and *Englishman's Greek Concordance of the New Testament*. Both use Strong's numbers.

Don't cut and paste endless dictionary entries from some electronic resource. The goal of a word study is for *you* to make a dictionary. A word won't mean all those meanings every place it is used. You are trying to find the one meaning the word has in each of the passages you are interested in. A one or two word start is as good as ten full Greek dictionary entries.

2. If you are looking at a specific passage, brainstorm what nuance you think the word might have in that immediate context. This is just a rough draft to get you started.

3. Now look at the other places in that book where the word (or phrase) is used. Start a list of different meanings the word can have (don't mix them together).

You will need to find out all the places where the word or phrase is used. For this task, an English concordance will not work. An English concordance tells you everywhere a word appears in a particular English translation like the KJV or NIV.

It will not work for two reasons. First, the same English word often translates into more than one word in the original language. If you are meaning to study a particular word in a particular verse, an English concordance causes you to study other words as well without even realizing it. The mistake some make in thinking there is only one meaning for a word is called the *one meaning fallacy*.

Second, a word in one language almost always has more than one possible meaning in another. If you only look at the English word, you might miss half the places where that word appears in the original.

To find all the places in the Old or New Testament where a Hebrew or Greek word appears if you do not have a Greek or Hebrew concordance, you will want to use the resources we mentioned above under step 1. Blueletterbible.com works well for this purpose, as does *Young's* or *Englishman's Concordance*. Many software packages give you all the resources you can imagine (e.g., *Logos* software or *BibleWorks*).

4. Now look at any other places the word might occur in any other books by the same author. As necessary, expand

Word Study: Conscience

Starting Point: Hebrews 9:14—"How much more, then, will the blood of Christ . . . cleanse our consciences from acts that lead to death, so that we may serve the living God!"

Interpretive Question: What does the word *conscience* mean in this verse?

Greek Word: *syneidisis*

Brainstorming (Immediate Context):

- *Conscience* contrasts with *flesh* in 9:13. The blood of bulls and goats sanctifies flesh; the blood of Christ, offered through eternal spirit, cleanses our conscience. So whatever conscience is, it contrasts with flesh.
- The conscience is cleansed "from dead works." Are these sins?
- The cleansing of the conscience enables a person to serve the living God.

Other Instances in Hebrews:

9:9 "This is an illustration for the present time, indicating that the gifts and sacrifices being offered were not able to clear the *conscious* of the worshiper" (emphasis mine). This verse is very similar to 9:14, especially since Levitical sacrifices are called *requirements of flesh*.

10:2 With the same sacrifices that they offer continually they are never able to perfect those who approach, since would they not have stopped offering them otherwise because they would not still have *conscience* of sins, once the worshipers had been cleansed. The meaning of *syneidisis* in this verse is fairly clear, since the word *consciousness* makes for a much better translation. Conscience is thus that part of the mind that is aware of having sins not atoned for. Perhaps this conscience is aware of other things as well, but it is at least aware of whether you are cleansed of sins or not.

10:22 "Let us draw near to God with a sincere heart in full assurance of faith having our hearts sprinkled to cleanse us from a guilty *conscience* and having our bodies washed with pure water" (emphasis mine). In the light of what precedes, a "guilty conscience" is surely an awareness of unforgiven sins.

13:18 "Pray for us. We are sure that we have a clear *conscience* and desire to live honorably in every way" (emphasis mine). A conscience here would again seem to be a sense of whether you have done right or wrong. The author does not indicate that a person's conscience is always correct in its assessment, but it is apparently that faculty that is either aware or unaware of wrongdoing.

Summary: All of the instances of *syneidisis* in Hebrews seem to involve an awareness or consciousness of uncleansed sins. It appears, therefore, that the word means *awareness of* something.

Other occurrences in the New Testament: Although our study of Hebrews alone has largely answered our initial question, a full word study would now look at all the other places where the word is used in the New Testament, using the same process of study: Acts 23:1; 24:16; Romans 2:15; 9:1; 13:5; 1 Corinthians 8:7, 10, 12; 10:25, 27–29; 2 Corinthians 1:12; 4:2; 5:11; 1 Timothy 1:5, 19; 3:9; 4:2; 2 Timothy 1:3; Titus 1:15; 1 Peter 2:19; 3:16, 21.

Further Study: To create a complete Greek dictionary entry for this word, you would want to look at every place in Greek literature where it occurs. In terms of Hebrews, you might first look at all the places where the Greek word occurs in the Septuagint, the Greek translation of the Old Testament used at the time of Christ. Then you use the *Thesaurus Linguae Graecae* to look up all the instances in ancient literature where the word occurred. More helpful is to seek out an original meaning commentary on Hebrews. If the author of it has done his or her homework, they should clue you into any important aspects of this word in the Greco-Roman world.

your list of possible meanings the word can have. You are creating a range of possible meanings and making your own dictionary.

5. For historical background, look at the rest of the places where that word is used by other authors of that day. Start with the rest of the New Testament if you are studying a Greek word. Look at the Greek Old Testament if you are doing a New Testament word. If it seems like a New Testament author is building on some Old Testament passage, focus on it. But if the author isn't using the Hebrew Bible, it is really irrelevant to bring in the meaning of the Hebrew original. It is not at all certain that a New Testament author

will pay any attention to the original context of an Old Testament word or passage.

Look at the rest of the Old Testament if you are doing a Hebrew word. But don't look at the New Testament for the original meaning of an Old Testament word. That is a path to anachronism.

As much as you are able, and as information is available, explore how the word or phrase was used in the secular writings of the day. How did secular Greek speakers use the word *gospel*? What ancient Near Eastern literature might give hints about the meaning of *leviathan*?

6. Now return to the passage in question. From the dictionary you have created, select a meaning for your passage that seems best to fit its immediate context.

As you try to hone in on the meaning of a particular word, avoid the word fallacies we have mentioned along the way: the overload, anachronistic, and one meaning fallacies. We should mention a few other common word fallacies as well before we end the topic of word studies.

The *etymological fallacy* is when you assume that the history of a word has something to do with the meaning of a word today. For example, the Greek word for church, *ekklesia*, comes historically from two shorter words: *ek*, meaning "out of," plus *kaleo,* "to call." You will often hear preachers saying then that the church consists of those who are the "called out" ones.

But no New Testament author would have thought about this history any more than we think about the fact that the word *understand* comes from *under* plus *stand*. In fact, the word *ekklesia* is used for an angry mob in Acts 19:41. This is a fine sermon illustration of the church if you tell your congregation you are only making an illustration. But it has nothing to do with the original meaning of the word *church* in the New Testament.

Another closely related mistake is the *root fallacy*. The root fallacy is when you assume that some core meaning of a word plays itself out in all the instances where that word appears. But the different meanings of a word need not have any relationship to one another whatsoever. For example, the word *archo* means *to rule* in one form and *to begin* in another. Don't try to find some core, essential meaning behind both. Words just mean different things in different contexts.

Finally, interpreters sometimes link an idea to a particular word. If they can't find this word, then they assume the idea isn't present either. But just because the book of Esther doesn't mention God does not necessarily mean that its author did not believe in God. Or just because Deuteronomy doesn't use the word for graciousness very often doesn't necessarily mean that it doesn't have a sense of God's graciousness. Concepts are not limited to the use of a specific word, so this is sometimes called the *word-concept fallacy*.

SUMMARY OF INTERPRETIVE METHOD

We are now in a position to summarize the process of arriving at the original meaning of a biblical text.

1. Come to the text prepared! You have prayed for the illumination of your mind and have honed your skills of observation both for the big picture and for the details.

2. Take a careful look at the immediate context of the passage you want to interpret. Brainstorm without closing your mind.

3. Now go to the broader literary context. Gather evidence. You might even make two columns: one for evidence and the other for possible conclusions—what you think that evidence implies (see chart). If you are studying a word, see how that word is used in the broader context. Consider the genre of the book or passage in question.

4. Now go to the historical background. Where does this book or passage fit in the flow of history and culture? How would Joe Ancient have likely heard these words? Look at other books by the same author if you can find any.

5. Now go back to the immediate context of the passage and lay out the most likely train of thought given all the evidence you have gathered.

Evidence	Possible Conclusions
11:25 refers to a part of Israel that has experienced a hardening until the full number of the Gentiles come in.	Since this is the immediate context, it is difficult to think that this is not the Israel Paul has in mind in 11:26. • In 11:25, a part is hardened and a part presumably is not. In 11:26, all Israel is saved. • In 11:25, the hardening of a part is temporary, waiting until the full number of the Gentiles enters in. So it makes sense that 11:26 is the softening after they come in.
11:28–29 also refers to this Israel's current status as enemies in relation to the Gentiles, but also says God's election is irrevocable.	This mirrors what we saw in number one above: • A contrast between Israel now (enemies) and then (saved). • The election of Israel most naturally refers to the Old Testament covenant (see Deut. 7:6–9). Even though they are currently enemies, God will not go back on his election of them.

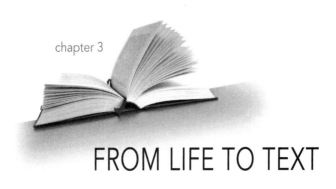

chapter 3

FROM LIFE TO TEXT

EXPERIENCE

More than anything else, our experiences of life drive us to seek a word from God. Our search for direction and our drive to make sense of it all pushes us to search for a word. A loved one is diagnosed with cancer or is killed in a car accident. We lose our job. A family member announces that she is homosexual. Perhaps a minister needs a word to bring to a congregation on Sunday. Our experiences often set the agenda for our approach to the Bible.

This is the case even when we are not in crisis mode. Our experiences of the world significantly affect what we see and what we don't see as we approach the text. It determines what questions are most on our minds. Our skills of observation help us see more than what is on our conscious minds; they can self-critique what is on our minds in relation to the text. But experience tends to set the agenda.

To be sure, countless aspects of our experience are prone to lead us away from a true word from God as we read the Scripture. Sometimes we don't want the word from God that we need. We don't want to hear that we can't hate our enemy. Experience teaches us that it's dangerous to give a second chance to those who've hurt us.

But when we are in tune with the Holy Spirit, experience can also provide spiritual common sense that helps us think God's thoughts. For example, Scripture does not provide a clear statement allowing a battered wife to depart from her husband. But surely a God of love would not insist she stay with a man who may one day kill her. It goes against every Christian intuition we have, especially when we consider that Jesus did not model an exception-less approach to rules.

Or take a passage like 1 Corinthians 11 on women wearing coverings when they pray or prophesy in church. It's difficult to follow the logic of this passage, try as we might. When we turn to the scholarly literature, we find a good deal of disagreement and diversity of explanation. These are telltale signs that the specifics of this passage, both in content and argument, are so intertwined with the circumstances and culture of the first century that they do not translate directly to today.

It is highly doubtful that a Christian home can operate like the household codes of 1 Peter and accomplish the same goal it had in the first century. That goal was to have such good conduct among the Gentiles that, while they speak against you as a criminal, they will glorify God on the Day of Visitation because they have seen your good deeds (see 1 Pet. 2:12). In the ancient world, a well-ordered home with the woman in her place was a respectable home and a good witness. But in our world, to limit the role a woman can play in society is probably not a good witness. Rather, it seems to contradict the message God calls us to proclaim: oppression, inequality, superiority. We can put forward finely tuned arguments that it is not oppression, for example, but the world will still perceive it this way. The message of 1 Peter at this point was more about witnessing to the oppressive world around it than about setting out a timeless theology or ideology. Our generation will not glorify God with a good witness when we place boundaries around women simply because their bodies are different from men's bodies.

The most difficult question is to know when the Holy Spirit is witnessing to our spirit or when we are misguided and listening to our flesh. Here we must submit (not surrender) to larger forces. There are individual prophets who are called to go against the grain. We must always have a place for them among us. But we will know a prophet by whether the call catches on and grows, or dies with him or her.

Beyond the spiritual sense of one individual is the collective spiritual sense of a group. It holds greater authority and is more likely to represent God's will. Still greater authority has the collective spiritual sense of a generation, and still greater the consensus of Christians throughout the century. We assume that all these individuals and groups are in dialogue with Scripture—the place where all such discussions begin and the playing field on which the dialogues of application are conducted.

But we cannot ignore the role thinking and experience play both in the movement from text to life and from life to text. The Bible is not some third path to truth—it is our *first source* of truth, but it is not a path to truth that bypasses our normal paths of reasoning. All the things that we think are true must pass through our individual reasoning and experience. There is no way around it; we are stuck in our heads.

THE SENSE OF THE CHURCH

Most of us who grew up going to church have likely absorbed more than we might think. We have picked up the rules for how and how not to apply the biblical text. Many Christians talk about the idea of the Bible alone, but they are unaware of the degree to which they bring these rules with them. Give a Bible to a person who knows nothing of Jesus or Christianity and send him or her away to read it. Apart from a miracle of the Holy Spirit, that same person will likely come back ready to start a cult.

Christians throughout the centuries have exercised spiritual common sense. One person's prophetic sense of the Holy Spirit can turn out to be authoritative, but imagine the collective spiritual sense as it has been tried and tested for two thousand years! That doesn't mean that the collective church cannot ever be wrong. Those of us who are Protestants believe that some of the correctives of the Protestant Reformation were right on track.

This sense of the one holy, universal, and apostolic church is found most noticeably in the common creeds of Christendom, the Apostle's Creed, the Nicene Creed, and the Athanasian Creed. These creeds ironed out issues like the Trinity and the nature of Christ's divinity (the essential dogma of historic Christendom). But even beyond these creeds are beliefs that are commonly held by almost all who have historically called themselves Christians: the belief that God created the world out of nothing and the belief that we begin our reward and punishment at death even before the resurrection. These ideas have been held in common as the consensus of the church even though none of the universal creeds say them.

These beliefs constitute the rule of faith and set boundaries for how we appropriate (not interpret) the biblical text. Evangelicals have tended to use their intelligence and skill to make their interpretations of Scripture come out to teach these things. However, this tendency sets up a kind of paradox in which a particular view of the biblical text—meant to elevate the value of the text—leads one to not listen to the text in deference to one's theology.

A far more honest method is to let the text mean what it meant and then acknowledge that there is a flow of revelation that moved not only from the Old to the New Testaments but also into the church as well. We have already discussed these dynamics in our section on hermeneutics.

So the rule of faith, the consensus of the church, stands as a boundary for how we can appropriate the teaching of the Bible. We must always allow for prophets like Martin Luther. These individuals prevent the church from having to justify beliefs that have been commonly held in the past, but which are now seen as phases of history, or even inappropriate trajectories. For example, there was a time when it was the consensus of Christendom that ministers should not marry. This may have been appropriate for the medieval phase of Christendom, but it seems problematic today as a universal rule. In situations like these, the original meaning of Scripture can play a crucial role in the debate, as it did in the Protestant Reformation.

If the rule of faith provides the rules for belief, the law of love constitutes the rule and boundary for ethics and action. The law that a believer should do nothing that contradicts love of God and neighbor has the dominant hand in the New Testament, affirmed by Jesus (Matt. 22:34–40), Paul (Rom. 13:8–10), James (2:8), and John (1 John 4:7–8). It has also been reaffirmed by prophets of the church such as Augustine.

These two rules form boundaries for how we can appropriate Scripture. Our appropriations must cohere with the rule of faith, the consensus of the church as regards our beliefs. They must also cohere with the royal law of love. No appropriation of Scripture that is inconsistent with love of God or neighbor can be properly considered Christian.

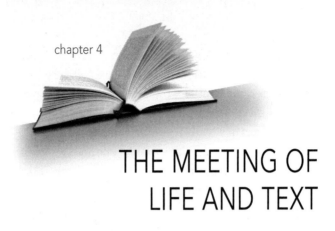

chapter 4

THE MEETING OF LIFE AND TEXT

INTEGRATION

The most crucial element in integrating biblical teaching on any matter is finding the appropriate place to stand — finding a center from which to synthesize the individual teachings of Scripture. This Archimedian point will largely determine how you prioritize, emphasize, and de-emphasize various passages in relation to each other. As we previously mentioned, it is important for us to acknowledge that the Bible cannot tell us where this point is. It is a matter of theology we bring to the text, not a matter of the text itself. Here we suggest some of the Christian theological presuppositions that are in play as we try to integrate biblical teaching.

New Testament Governs Old

It would be theoretically possible, particularly for an orthodox Jew, to read the Christian Bible that includes what we, today, call the New Testament as an aberration from the authoritative Jewish Bible that Christians call the Old Testament. Thus when Paul suggests that he is not "under the law" in 1 Corinthians 9:20, it would be perfectly possible for a person to suggest that he is deviating from the authoritative law of Genesis, Exodus, Leviticus, Numbers, and Deuteronomy.

But from a Christian perspective, the New Testament provides an authoritative lens through which to read the Old Testament. New Testament passages thus take priority when integrating New Testament teaching with Old. For example, in the flow of revelation, most of the Old Testament is not yet aware of any personal, conscious life after death. One psalmist says, "No one remembers you when he is dead. Who praises you from the grave?" (Ps. 6:5). Yet for the New Testament, belief in resurrection is essential to Christian faith. In this case, and others like it, the New Testament takes the governing role in relation to the appropriation of the Old Testament.

There is probably a sense in which this governance applies to the meaning of the Old Testament as well. In previous sections of this guide, we have pointed out how Matthew's appropriations of verses like Isaiah 7:14 and Hosea 11:1 vary significantly from the original meanings of these same passages. The New Testament writers almost always redirect the meaning of the Old Testament in some way (some more than others).

Therefore, the Hebrew Bible (the Jewish Bible) is, in a sense, pre-Christian—the meanings these words had in their original contexts. We should respect the original meanings of these texts. Evangelicals will want to consider these inspired revelations for the specific contexts to which they were directed at specific points in the overall flow of revelation. But there is also a sense in which these texts are only authoritative over us today as the Old Testament—the significance these words have taken on in the light of the New Testament and the subsequent church.

The Kingdom of God

The key to integrating New Testament teaching is to determine what the kingdom perspective is on any issue. In other words, what will God's ideal world look like? With regard to matters of ethics, the New Testament already has as its prevalent principle the love of God and the love of neighbor as the absolute principles of New Testament ethics. Any appropriation of biblical ethics that we can show does not fit with these principles is inappropriate. Care must be taken in light of the fact that some are prone to consider unloving that which is not truly unloving. For example, it is not unloving to carry out justice, even if love tends toward mercy.

The kingdom perspective is not identical to Christ's perspective in the Gospels or in some abstracted historical Jesus. The earthly Jesus directed his teaching not at the whole world but at Israel, and mostly Galileans at that. Secondly, the gospel writers each presented Jesus with special emphases to address late first-century audiences.

In that sense, the gospel presentations of Jesus are as much expressions of the theologies of Matthew, Mark, Luke, and John as they are videotapes of things Jesus did and said. We have already mentioned some of the contrasting impressions they give. So, for the most part we should consider Paul's teachings to have the same level of authority that they have.

The kingdom perspective is an end times (eschatological) perspective. It asks where the biblical texts seem to indicate God will eventually lead the world, particularly after Christ's return. For example, in the kingdom there will be no differentiation between male and female. Galatians 3:28 already announces this spiritual principle, even if various New Testament texts retain the distinctions that were current in Paul's day. Integrating the biblical teaching requires us to determine which appropriation will apply to the kingdom and whether there are any earthly reasons to stop short of them now when it is possible to enact them.

The question of women's role in the home and church is a good illustration of the process of integrating biblical teaching on a subject, and we have already said much on this issue. In this process, Galatians 3:28 provides a spiritual principle that in Christ, "there is neither . . . male nor female." Both men and women are equally children of God. We recognize in other eschatological, end times passages that in the age of the Spirit, both men and women will prophesy (e.g., Acts 2:17). How then do we integrate these principles with the teaching of the household codes of Colossians 3:18 or 1 Peter 3:1–6, where we find a hierarchy of authority in the home? How do we integrate these principles with 1 Timothy 2:12, which at the very least seems to ban a wife from teaching her husband? This is the question of biblical integration, finding the biblical center on the issue, which, again, is as much a matter of our theology as of the Bible itself.

It is at this point that we must take context closely into consideration. In our view, the contexts of passages like Galatians 3:28 and Acts 2:17 are eschatological, kingdom contexts. They tell us where history is headed, as Jesus implies in the Synoptic Gospels when he proclaims that women are not given in marriage—are not subordinated to husbands—in the kingdom of God. On the other hand, passages like Colossians 3 and 1 Peter 3 fit perfectly with what pagan writers like Aristotle had to say about the order of the household, with their cultural context. We can easily place these passages against the backdrop of a church that stands in a defensive posture with its world.

Our integration of the biblical teaching on the woman's role in the home and church thus sees passages like Acts 2 and Galatians 3 as the governing principles while other passages like Colossians 3 and 1 Timothy 2 are time-bound to specific ancient contexts. We need not deny their authority for their specific contexts to see them as concessions to particular times and places. Key is that we let each passage mean what it meant without twisting one to force it to fit with the other. True integration does not make one fit with the other, but prioritizes the one in relation to the other.

Center Points in the Church

When it comes to matters of ethics, the twin ethic to love God and neighbor provides a center point from which to integrate biblical instructions in the light of contemporary contexts. But there are other topics on which the New Testament has not yet reached a final answer. In such cases, we should integrate the biblical teaching in the light of the rule of faith that has arisen in the later church and listen keenly to the prophetic voices among us.

So it is in the light of subsequent Christian history that we recognize Hebrews as the governing text on the matter of sacrifice. The Old Testament would not lead us to see any end to literal sacrifice. The bulk of the New Testament is not incompatible with the continuance of blood sacrifices. Hebrews has been long since recognized as the final answer on whether continued blood sacrifices are necessary, and Christians have recognized this fact without even realizing how controversial it would have been to the earliest Christians.

Yet Hebrews does not fit easily with the rule of faith on the question of second repentance. Can a person use up Christ's sacrifice for sin in such a way that he or she can never find a place of repentance again? Hebrews seems to say so (10:26; 12:17). Yet the Christian consensus has long been much more in tune with 1 Corinthians 5:5, where a person can be turned over to Satan with the hope of his or her future salvation still intact. The later rule of faith pushes us to consider passages of this latter sort more governing than those of Hebrews on this topic.

We see in the above discussion the reason why we have placed the subject of integration in the section on life meeting the text. The task of integration ultimately stands at the heart of fusing our lives with Scripture. The two rules of appropriation—the rule of faith and the law of love—stand at the heart of the process of integration. The biblical and ethical principle of love must stand as the governing element in the equation of any biblical instruction. True love of God cannot truly contradict true love of my neighbor. At the same time, we recognize that life will never be fair while we are in this fallen world, and God wills sometimes by concession rather than by the ideal.

When it comes to the rule of faith, the New Testament governs the Old. When the New Testament teaching was still in process, the consensus of Christians everywhere was to indicate where to center our prioritization of New Testament material. What we are ultimately seeking here is the kingdom perspective on any given topic. As best we can, we seek to enact God's will on earth as it is in heaven, recognizing that our specific contexts and situations will often prevent us from the ideal.

APPROPRIATION

And so we finally arrive at the ultimate goal of this process: appropriating God's Word today.

From Text to Life

Although in actual practice we are more likely to come to the biblical text from our lives, we have also created a process by which someone might move from text to life. We set out this linear process that begins with prayer, followed by accurate observation. This leads to correct interpretations of the original meanings and is followed by the integration of biblical teaching by prioritizing and organizing the varied individual material of the Bible. The final step in this text-to-life process is the appropriation of this integrated perspective to our lives.

An integrated understanding of the biblical witness is already most of the way to a good appropriation of the biblical text. The process of finding a biblical center already requires us to bring a Christian theological perspective to the biblical text. We have determined the relation of Old Testament teaching to New, and we have considered the place of the New Testament in relation to the overall flow of revelation into the church. We have abstracted overarching principles in relation to the Bible as a whole. Finally, we have attempted to determine what the Bible affirms on whatever topics the text has generated for us (or that we have brought to the text searching for answers).

Before we appropriate this theological center, we might double check two matters one more time. First, we should examine the degree of continuity and discontinuity between their time and our time. How does our current situation and culture compare and contrast with the situations and cultures of the key passages we have looked at in this process? If we have identified Christian love, hospitality, and friendship as biblical principles, would a holy kiss promote this in our context as it did in that of the ancient Mediterranean world? Or might some other form of greeting better accomplish those goals today? Sometimes discontinuity implies that less or more ethical requirements apply and sometimes the ethical expectation will simply be something different.

Second, where do we stand in the flow of revelation? Where has God led the church universal on this topic? Are there any prophetic movements afoot that seem to have a future? What is the kingdom trajectory? I believe that one such prophetic movement since the 1800s has been that of women in ministry. There are clear biblical and theological precedents for it, and it has only gained increasing support this past century. As with various features of the Protestant Reformation, history will make it clear in hindsight that God was in this movement in the church.

From Life to Text

Coming to the biblical text from our lives is like sitting down at a table with a group of wise counselors, a table of discernment and inspiration. By the nature of the situation, you are the one who must carry the word from the table. The chair of the committee is the Holy Spirit. We long for this Holy Guest to make the final decision, to go with us as we take the word into life.

But you are the one forced to take that decision from the table. We will not always be sure that we have correctly heard what God is saying to us. This fact calls for great humility as interpreters and appropriators of Scripture. We do our best to hear his will. But then we must take responsibility for our understanding. This is why it is safest for us to read the Bible in a community of faith rather than as lone individuals. If the Spirit inhabits the body of Christ, then we are more likely to hear the Spirit accurately if we have more of the body of Christ listening with us.

So the committee chair's seat is reserved for the Holy Spirit. But you have many other counselors seated at the table with you. The original meanings of all the individual biblical texts are there. Seated with them are their assistants: good observation and interpretation. Experience and spiritual common sense are also at the table to help you hear the Spirit. Sometimes the Spirit assumes their seats and speaks prophetically and authoritatively through them.

The common understandings of Christians throughout the ages are there as well, especially the law of love and the rule of faith. Next to you is the trusted advisor, the integration of Scripture made under the counsel of the timeless church. This advisor is the one most likely to help you hear God's authentic word, the voice of the Holy Spirit.

The word of God is bigger than any written word or formula. Any life decision will involve the whole council of God. Which voice will speak loudest on any one occasion is God's business and cannot be reduced to a pat answer. The goal is to hear the voice of God for today, for now, for this moment.

Another picture of this process is that of a group of builders who know how to use the word of truth correctly. God is using this group, the church, to build his kingdom. It has at its disposal all the tools that we have discussed: skills of observation, interpretation, and integration; knowledge of the rule of faith and a heart filled with the law of love; and spiritual common sense. The Holy Spirit is the contractor who enacts the plans of the Father. The tools that are needed for each part of the construction will differ.

Appropriating the Scriptures is a spiritual art. It's true that "X" does not always mark the spot. The ways that Jesus and Paul appropriated Scripture were not always literalist or always allegorical. It varied. Sometimes it was absolutist, but more often it was contextual. It was spiritual and, in some cases, unpredictable.

Nevertheless, the appropriation of Scripture for today must always cohere with the two core principles. First, it must always cohere with an absolute love of God and of our fellow neighbor. Any appropriation that is driven by the hatred of others is unchristian and unworthy of Christ. Secondly, the appropriation of Scripture should be in continuity with the communion of the saints throughout the ages. Although God does direct prophetic movements in the church, beliefs and practices outside the commonly held beliefs and practices of Christians throughout the ages are unlikely to be of God. The burden of proof will always lie with the new. It is hardly possible to reject wholesale some two thousand years of Christian history without rejecting to some significant degree the God that they and the authors of the Bible worshiped.

The Bible as Scripture is thus much bigger than the original meaning. Yet it is also vastly bigger than the way the words might strike us on a given day. To be sure, the Holy Spirit can speak authoritatively to us through Scripture however he wills. But as a rule, the most authoritative meaning of Scripture is the meaning these words have taken on as they have been read by the saints of all the ages, a canonical meaning in the fullest sense of that term. God led the church to recognize the boundaries of the canon, and God has led the church to hear boundaries in its appropriation. It is the ongoing task of the universal church to seek out these meanings, as well as to apply and reapply them to our lives.